THE FRAGILE CAVE

Poems inspired by the cavers
and caves of Britain

Elise Freshwater-Blizzard

The Fragile Cave

For information contact :

elisefreshwater-blizzard@yahoo.co.uk

Book Formatting by Derek Murphy @Creativindie

Book and Cover design by © 2020 Rae Robinson

Author Photo by Tim Dobson

With thanks to Gale Freshwater

ISBN: 978-1-83853-267-3

First Edition: May 2020

10 9 8 7 6 5 4 3 2 1

Preface

I wrote this collection in a negative space in my life. Seasonal depression had hit hard, I felt alone, and felt I was not being the person I really wanted to be. Having drawn out a mental-health plan, I was determined to build my life into something that gave me more meaning and self-love.

Throughout this time, I found solace in writing down poetry about caves and cavers, since my primary hobby at the University of Sheffield is caving in the Peak District, a twenty-minute drive from Sheffield. In time, my poems became more self-accepting and grounded as I became happier with life, and what I have forged over time.

In this body of work, the cave represents the nature of the human mind. The idea of Mother Nature strung throughout this book is most important. It is the unstoppable force of nature that decides our path for us, which is why I framed cave rescue as 'angels' trying to work against what mother nature had, unfairly, 'chosen'. Even with the callout person described in 'Schrödinger's Cat' is described with the same adjectives popularly used to describe God. This is the battle between Fate and 'deus ex machina'- the intervention from godly beings.

In the end, the missing cat from the first poem is sadly still lost in: 'Mother Red in Tooth and Claw.' Our story closes with the idea that: there are some things in life that we cannot change- and sometimes the ones we love the most, must move away from us. However, we should let this be. Furthermore, this should never stop us from going out into the world ourselves for our own journey of self-love and improvement. There is always room to be more at peace with our life and cherish the memories we were given.

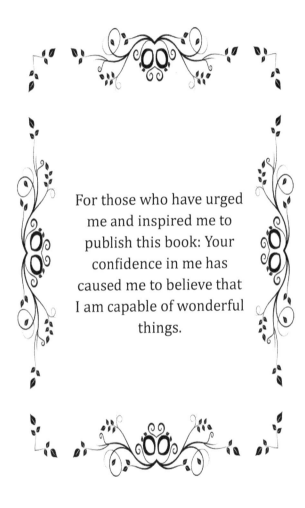

For those who have urged
me and inspired me to
publish this book: Your
confidence in me has
caused me to believe that
I am capable of wonderful
things.

Contents

Missing

-Brown fur

-Hazel eyes

-Last seen outside peak cavern.

Please contact me if you have seen my cat.

peak cavern is a famous tourist cave in the Peak District

Water

Do you know how the greatest caves are made?

it is the water that hits the rock

carrying carbon dioxide

carving out limestone

water falling across fields

and running into streams

towards the rocky land

that carves out over time

I like to call it 'Pressure'.

the small amounts of pressure from water onto rock

chisels, chisels..

away

over

time

water will always find the quickest and easiest route through the rock

Direct.

Non-hesitant.

sometimes, cutting too deep.

sometimes, too much pressure.

but this will always make the cave far grander than before.

So-much-so, that folk may tell tales of its caverns.

So I ask you-

What pressures have you had lately?

Is the cave of your life more lavish and intricate than before?

How many walkways and secret paths might there be by now?

And how many more paths do you think there will be if you

let the water

run

run

run

down

through your mind

and into your sumps of subconsciousness?

- don't ignore the pressure or try and stop the water that creates the workings of your inner mind-

Let it

run

run

run

as it will always find its

Sump*

in the end.

*A sump is a hollow at the bottom of the cave, where water collects itself.

Caves before people

peace sat inside holes-

Noisy, chattering cavers.

Then, the caves LIT UP!

The time we went caving

Do you remember the time we went caving?

The cold wind whipped around our necks as we stuffed our clustered baggage into the car, seats full to the brim, cherry faces hidden within the sea of blue and yellow oversuits*.

Do you remember the time we went caving?

Empty carpark, paying our dues firmly to the farmer as he glances at the grim faces in the backseat, returning to the warmth of his den. Wheezing of breath from the tug of the Wellington boot, clanging of Cowstails* as we strap ourselves in for the journey.

Do you remember the time we went caving?

The stiff march as we pound our feet, already caked in ice and stiff mud, our breath spewing into the night air. The beady eyes of the sheep that mock us in their thick coats as our lights cut through the darkness. Our already shivering hands, whimpering in the black and blue evening, the last tinge of orange had set for the night.

Do you remember the time we went caving?

Tucked away, a frozen entrance, cut deep into the darkness of the hillside, standing solitary. Fearlessly frozen in the night. A tiny locked entrance into a different world, beckons us in, like honey to pooh-bear. We make haste and fall towards the entrances' dark allure. And upon the rusted gate:

"

- Do you have the keys?

-no- no, I th-thought you..you had them?

"

Pure panic pounds within us as we collectively stare into the grey abyss that is the cold, hard entrance, with a hole that had no key. We are cavers with no cave. The pools of our eyes, shrinking in grief from the adventure that cannot be. What times we might have had? Stuffing our over-fed bodies into tiny cracks, to discover what would have been. But like an untouched stalagmite, stubborn to the touch: our stiff bodies refusing to note that the key might be easily retrieved if we desired it so. We begin to cast our eyes on each other. A smile begins to curve between our teeth- the unspoken words that flash between us as we glance back and forth, between the now hearty breaths in the air.

"

-Pub?

-Go on then.

"

And we settle down back into the belly of warmth and light, stripped bare of old sagging undersuit. Consuming ourselves in golden brews that fill our stomachs with the joy of a thousand warm summer days, within the deep cocoon of soft chatters and deep conversations with our caving family. And when they ask us, lo,

"How was your caving trip?"

We deceive them.

And when one shall ask:

"Do you remember the time we went caving"

We shall always answer;

"Yes, Yes Indeed I do."

*

Oversuits: cavers wear protective oversuits underground

Cowstails: instruments attached to one's harnesss for safety when dealing with rope work.

A caving poem
for lovers

The mud that sits on your cheeks

As you smile the soft smile you always do

We could just sit on the peaks

Or be at the bottom of Ogof Ffynnon Ddu*

These are the moments I know I love you.

Deep within the surveys of Peak Cavern,

together as we sing in the dead of night

we would each slowly take our turn

to overpower the cold waters with love and
might

And I may not be the best caver, I'm ashamed
my step may not be like yours, quick and agile
but you take comfort in my joy untamed,
and help me feel confident once again.

If you could love me, the way you do
throwing the mud in my face playfully,
Perhaps then, I could love myself too,
and spend my time underground more joyfully

    The Titan* of heights,
    The Perryfoot* of squeezes,
    The mud-fight of all fights
    So many things love teaches.
    I could conquer all my fears just to see

how powerful I could really be

with you right there holding my hand

to create a space for you and me

So take me down to the deepest boulder choke

and whisper those engraved fears

Dark ones for only me, or lighter for your kins-folk:

Like how you lost your torch at the bottom of Swildon's sump*– now on the verge of tears

as pressures of cold rocks press against on your neck

because what we're afraid of is death

but I have always known you

and let it be true

that you and I can both make it with anything this world has left

and I will comfort you through and through

because in the end when I feel all my emotions
bereft

and you comfort me as you do,

These are the moments I know I love you.

And I know it won't be perfect,

but there will be perfection found:

There will be light within the darkness

And blood within stone

The diamonds at the exit

Your smile in my pocket.

And if you are ever in doubt, I'll repeat such a
poem, until your heart is lit up with the lights
of a thousand show caves, with visitors' pris-
tine feet stumbling into, so that they may gaze
upon in awe:

The mud that sits on your cheeks

As you smile the soft smile you always do

We could just sit on the peaks

Or be at the bottom of Ogof Ffynnon Ddu

These are the moments I know I love you.

*

Ogof Ffynnon Ddu: The deepest cave in the UK

Titan: The deepest shaft in the UK. 141.5 meters tall

Perryfoot: A cave known for its small spaces

Sump: A passage of cave submerged in water, often dived by cave divers

Blue John Stone*

John, he was named

and for Blue he was famed

but in his appearance, untamed

blue was not to be found.

For his eyes spoke a better hazed purple,

with the whites around them lying.

I had heard those lies before

wrapped in those ever-expanding circles.

They encompassed his wide and wild night sky

with thick purple dusted memories glimmering

against hot white stars of his past,

that flashed and danced around the waves of

deep warm and light currents of thick purples;

lavender, magenta, wine and mulberry

that shrouded round those bright pin pricks

in a vast sea of dazed space that

if I swim in forever, I would only see less than

1%

of space and time in an endless drift.

I wanted to believe

when he turned to me and said

he'd see me again.

Just like I wanted to sit with him

and know how his young, exciting soft words

might taste of sweet port against my old ears

I wanted to know his path

His stars

His oceans

But Blue John was soft to the touch

so I believed his rolling tides of

Purple.

Easy to see but rare to feel

so of course,

I wanted to believe

but since he had left

I understood why John's name was wrapped in
blue:

his calming cool purple faded to a boring hue,

perhaps my expectations had drowned me before

reality made me realise that,

endlessness and timelessness is tiresome.

Once the ring sitting on the end of my finger

meant freedom

but now it was just another circle that grew

until it slipped off my soft nails and edged

to the dullest of grey

Blue John Stone: Only found in the peak district, is purple in colour

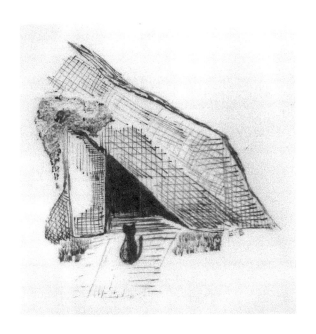

Cave.

I am the mist that rises forever,

I am the water that runs through the walls

I am the rock you pierce

the rope you climb

the light you shine onto the glimmering
depths of darkness

I am the muddy footsteps carved by cavers

I am the sweat that drips from your forehead
as you hook your Cowstails

But I am nothing.

I am nothing when you leave.

But I was always this way,

and will always

be

.

The Caveman's wife

15th February, 1997- set in a cold museum.

She stared at the plastic statue of a naked caveman. The mannequin, dull face, dangling arms draping the floor, and matted, white-speckled hair. The dull eyes and wooden club clasped firmly in hand. Teeth as shiny as wood, brown in stature and gum. Netted beard hanging down to the black chest. An ugly sight to behold.

She looked back at her husband and points at the statue

"My darling, look! *It's you*!"

And he responds

"Yes, because that's always been your type!".

Too many cooks

Every single caver put their suit on that day

And every caver entered the same cave

And every in the same hour's dismay

'How can it be?' you may ask

But every caver adventured fast

And questions like this were not asked

Ogof Fynnon Ddu filling up to the brim

Five thousand cavers were packed in

The same route, all followin'!

Finding each other with unexpected chats

First bumping into friends, then they all sat

To laugh with joy in one cavern whilst eating cave snacks

large cavern, there's plenty of food to go round

Everyone, huddled together, safe and sound

loud cavern, holding this crowd.

'Look at the beauty of the water', one states,

some are discussing their love for calcium carbonate

And others gather in groups to sing songs and contemplate

How on earth this happened in the first place!

Schrödinger's cat

Stubborn, some call him.

Anchored, we call him.

He waits, not in fear.

He waits, not in vain.

Every needle struck

in every caving hut

counting down the hours

would make a man say: 'fuck!'

But he waits.

He sits alone, tiresome.

We sit with him, cumbersome.

He waits, phone on desk,

Whilst anxious hearts pounds in chest.

But he does not stir,

Or quarrel, so you see.

This is a man in waiting

waiting for his friends to flee.

A mystery emergency is in his hands,

time slows down, and pressure too grand.

Yet he is patient.

He is kind.

He works in mysterious ways,

but does fate lie?

Hand on phone.

One hour to go.

"Does anyone know?

If it's a no-show?"

And yet he sits.

He sits in his chair,

half an hour passed.

The clock begins to stare.

...

'I hope the cat's alive in there!'

...

His hands reach phone slowly,

Feet rush out quickly,

Within the depths there is a shout

'We're going to miss callout*!'

10 minutes and the mind, led astray.

'Should he wait that extra five?

Or cop-out and ring the dial?'

He sits....

..

He waits.

...

The screen lights up!

Is all ok?

Confirming lips,

relaxed thoughts relieve fits

the mind can finally sit

And so, he goes to rest,

until another day,

when he has to stay dressed

'till the un-godly hours of dismay.

Because the callout was made

for 3AM

But he'll sit

and wait

until he is needed again.

Callout: A responsible person outside the cave will be instructed on a 'callout time' to phone cave rescue if there is no contact within an allotted time.

Too drunk!

Standing on the table

Surrounded by her friends

She confronts the drunken lot

Calling as far as her pipes lend

"I may not be the best caver you've ever heard of!

...But you *have* heard of me!

I do not live up to your expectations

I am just a caver, drunk and free!

I am sexy!

Rebellious!

Full of cheek!

I am positive!

Insightful!

I'm full of glee!

'Shut up and get down!'

You may say-

but you see, I will ignore

until dawn breaks the day

And I will sing a merry tune

And dance a little dance

Because I'm the merry caver

Caught in a caving trance

I'm hopping onto tables!

I'm climbing up the walls!

And when everyone gets naked,

I'll know I've seen it all!

I'm stuck in the squeeze machine!*

I'm spending on the Seddon!*

..I'm waking with a headache

If I go cave now, I'm a dead-un!

So stall the breakfast

'Cos I'm in a funk

for at this cave-fest

I got far too drunk!

*

The squeeze machine: a small box that can be made smaller, the aim of the game is to pass through until the smallest box is made.

Mr Seddon: is a travelling merchant who sells caving supplies

The travelling man

The travelling man,

The travelling man,

Everybody stops for the travelling man

He's done every cave in the black book?*

The one who knows is the travelling man!

The travelling man,

The travelling man,

Everybody stops for the travelling man

His equipment is the far best in town?

The one who knows is the travelling man!

The travelling man,

The travelling man,

Everybody stops for the travelling man

He's got the equipment, you've got a plan

The only one who knows is the travelling man

The travelling man,

The travelling man,

Everybody stops for the travelling man

You've got no money because you're a fan

The only one who knows is the travelling man!

The collection of the hardest caving trips in one book

The reason I don't have non-caving friends

"I love a good shower" they all tend to say.

But they've got it all wrong, for I will exclaim:

you've never had a shower before

unless you're icy cold

in the empty concrete caving hut

and it hurts to pull your Croll*

You've never had a shower before

until your toes are numb

your fingers do not bend

and your throat ceases to hum

You've never had a shower before

until you're longing for tea

to warm your insides

as you tend your bruised knees

You've never had a shower before

until your naked round your friends

you turn the TSG* pipes on

and to heaven it will send

Because the water is magic

seeping into your skin

and you tell yourself:

You will never cave again!

Croll: Equipment used for climbing ropes

TSG: a caving hut in the Peak District

I am lost!

At last,

I am lost!

Where no man has been lost before.

The twists and turns that never end, define

my choices down a road which only I choose.

Left may have been the road back to life

when unknowingly, right is the path I took

and life may have beckoned me back to light

but left dazing and distracted by every nook

wet grey walls folded over like envelopes

send messages of cold hugs, leading further in

but I squeeze myself through sodden rock

only to be beckoned by the same walls again

madness concocted in happiness as I wander
alone

down the cave I willed to go in, but I must ask;

is every step, one which cannot be undone?

as it seems to me that time tied me to its mast

Perhaps only down the streamway I can float

since going up would seem a higher risk of

finding out where I am within this maze

since no phone, no internet, or warm love

could convince me to find myself otherwise

I don't know where I am, but seeking silence

will I ever see the light of day again?

but I can find myself and soothe away worries:

finally I may rest with my one friend.

I am lost...

Oh god.

I am lost...

Where no man has been lost before.

The twists and turns that never end, define

guilt chases down a road which only I choose.

Left may have been the road back to surface

when unknowingly, right is the path I took

my stupidity with only having one light

left dizzied and flickering by every nook

sharp grey walls folded over like bear traps

to kill any man in foolishness and caving in

I squeeze myself through sodden cracks

only to be greeted by those damn walls again

Madness upon madness as my mind explodes alone

down in the depths of hell I created, I hate to ask;

must I care about the steps I don't care to be undone?

Because I despise for how time got me here in past.

Perhaps if I force myself back up the stream-way,

since going up would seem a higher chance of

freedom of this stupid maze I had created

since no phone, no internet, distractions or love

could convince me to stay in this darned place otherwise

I just want to leave in this disgusting silence,

will I ever see the light of day again?

If nobody finds me to soothe my worries

I will never rest because I have not one friend.

Cave Rescue

Angels are the ones we take comfort in,

All waiting by their holy pristine engines.

They are the ones that who give up their lie-in,

To fly out and create the happy endings

To battle God upfront and save our souls,

From mistakes we have made, with one phone call.

Long hours and life on the clock that edges past

Without them, the caving community would never last.

Thank you.

Intermittent letter

Dear Lisa,

My darling,

I'm so sorry-

it's so unfortunate that I cannot stay, so I will write this love letter instead.

I can't see the in-laws since I must flee, for my caving friends have callen me!

I'm sure your mother will rat on about me (again)

But I won't care because I'll be where I'm supposed to be

My dear, don't you see? I do love you very much

I just need to be away without form of notice ..

Because I need time for myself in the darkness

I'd say I love you again, but I can hear your anger through the page

"I just need to be with people my 'own age'"

Ok..

Because that's all I hear you say

That we are all 'man-childs', digging in holes that decay

So please tell your mother I'm not showing up to-day!

If they ask, just say..

I'm doing the laundry or I have come down with flu

-Or-

that I'd rather be in than darkness than to be with you.

For, I know, and we know, that's the honest truth

Isn't it?

Love John

P.S

I want a divorce.

Dear Lisa,
my darling,
I'm so sorry -
it's so unfortunate that I cannot stay, so I will write this love
letter instead.

I can't see the in-laws since I must flea, for my caving friends
have callen me!
I'm sure your mother will rat on about me (again)
But I won't care because I'll be where I'm supposed to be
My dear, don't you see? I do love you very much
I just need to be away without form & notice...
Because I need time for myself in the darkness

I'd say I love you again, but I can hear your anger through the page
"I just need to be with people my 'own age'"
ok...
Because that's all I hear you say
That we are all 'man-childs', digging in holes that decay
So please tell your mother I'm not showing up today!

If they ask, just say...
I'm doing laundry or have come down with flu
                    - or -
that I'd rather be in the darkness than to be with you.
For, I know, and we know, that's the honest truth
Isn't it?
Love John

    P.S. I want a divorce.

47

Claustrophobic.

Writhing, trying to squirm our bodies forward through the cave. The ceiling, touching my nose. I can feel your squashed body next to me. Sharp corners of the limestone are condensing in on us, lying flat.

We just have to make it to the next part of the cave and then it will be ok, it's right in front of us. If we crawl together to the next tunnel, almost in reach, then we'll have room to make it through to the next part of our long-awaited journey. But the tunnel ahead is so dark that my light cannot lead the way.

I thought you'd help, right?!

but you don't.

I don't know where it leads, but it's better than being here, squashed. I'm trying to get there, shining my light on my own. But all you do is calmly kiss my neck.

Why won't you please do something?

Please.

I love you.

I can't move, now covered in thick, black treacle surrounding my entire body, hot bones pressed against freezing stone. But I can feel your hand, fingers intertwined. The only good green thing left in these empty caverns is your heart. The slight murmur of your breath against the ceiling. You're here, but you're not with me.

Oh god.

Is this a   dream?

You slowly reach out and turn my light off with a sad smile.

"It's going to be ok" You whisper, calmly as I writhe in panic. Breath in turmoil.

I sharply flick my light back on and look again to the path onwards. without a sound, the tunnel ahead is blocked.

...Gone.

A large stone had fallen upon the path I wanted to forge with you, whilst my light was off.

No sound was made, impossibly silent.

No vibration was felt, impossibly deadly.

I want to scream, mouth wide open and lungs grasping for thick air, but grit and fear seal up my windpipes. For the path is now forever gone. It cannot be forced. It cannot be moved. There is no way. There is no way ahead.

And I realise, that the only way out is to wake up. But I must do so alone. Can't I stay? Can't I stay and writhe in these last moments with you? The mud now suffocating deep into my

ears.

throat.

mouth.

I can feel the grit between my teeth and taste the wild romance now soured, lost to my own cold and once heated, now stale, passion.

And If I wake up, I have wake up without you. I must leave you in the cave that cannot go. The trapped tunnel that we had created together. The sealed tomb of our once flowering romance. The hopes and dreams of future is now just the past: wrapped in tarred, suffocating mud that I poisoned with my own mind.

And he says this, calmly, as I suffocate on a closing ceiling, pressed against my dry lips, heart now bleeding within its shaking cage..

"We can only make this out alone. It's now your choice. Either I leave you here or you wake up right now."

It's a shame

It's such a shame that they enjoy the saltwater more,

When glassy water, ebbing through the darkness shines bright.

It's so sad that people *enjoy* white salt, seeping into cheeks,

Rather than grinning in the golden sumps together

But I must accept that the salty abrasive split wears me thin;

Whilst he rejects the Freshwater, who dearly loved him.

If things were this easy

a. "hey do you wanna go caving in the next hour?"

b. "Yeah, my wife says it's a great time of day to go and all my kit is perfectly clean"

a. "You mean, all that kit that's sold at a decent price because of the good demand for caving products?"

b. "Yeah! Oh by the way, there's no gate on this cave and the farmer says the carpark is now free!"

a. "Wow. But don't wear too much because it's going to be nice and warm inside!"

b. "ok!! I'm so excited to prusik. It's so much fun."

a. "also I'm bringing my phone in, in case we get stuck inside we can phone someone.

....

You know what?"

b. "What?"

a. *"Caving is pretty boring."*

Prusik: To use equipment to move up a rope

She.

To see the roof supports begin to crack
to breathe cold air that pierced her lungs
to realise that she alone does not lack
everything the man said he does not love-
those things in fact, keep her on track.

In time she grows, and turns over every rock
until there are none left to turn and hold
and stone splits from under her wet socks
and the ice sharpens the tug of her croll,
even when her helmet pulls on her long locks.

These things make her wiser to the sharp tongue
more so than he, who thinks he knows it all
she still practices every song that was sung

whilst he prances about like an ignorant fool

yet she used to let him put her on his rung

He easily cracks under the conflict and argues

When she learned to hold the pressure,

sitting soft in the palm of her hand.

But give enough time and the power of her comes to call-

And then she realises that she is – legendary -

She sets her own heights,

She has a list of squeezes,

There's nothing she can't do

Alone, if she pleases.

she sees clearly what to do

And she does not need explaining

she has the confidence,

perseverance,

and the hours of training

the late nights round the ropes

withered hands from hours prusiking*

she let herself raise her hopes

knowing she'll never do the rigging

days on end she wasn't good enough

until moments of clarity for it is unveiled

the unsurity of self-worth was tough

but today the evil thoughts had failed.

she realised that all she *needed* was a buff

and the attitude of a woman untamed.

And this is where the tale ends.

But do not think that her story is over.

No, it has actually just begun.

The time is now to perfect her changeovers*

And with caves, again, fall in love

Her passion is not poison

She is feeding her personal growth

The world against this woman?

False. she was just own greatest foe.

*Changeover: The process of switching from going up a rope to going down a rope

I'm ready.

Nobody will tell you when you are ready

roots holding onto helmet and old light off

but you will feel it under the layers of skin

holding you tight with creases of emotion

Nobody will tell you when you are ready

to take those limp steps back in darkness

but the wind will swim through your hair

and the dark valley will sink into your eyes

I believed that I'd never be ready

that the armchair was my new home

I believed that I could not accomplish

what the seeds of time had already sown.

Nobody will tell you when your blood

pumps through like cold icy sleet

as the curiosity of the old silence

will glance at you from the concrete

And diving back into the black

Face, deep in mud

Blood, deep in limestone

Calcite heart

Porcelain bones

Protected by passion

Moulded by stone

I am ready, in my own heart

To call me home.

Waiting in solitude

Running all this way,
slowly, getting closer towards you **ROPE FREE!**

Ebbing and flowing

Below I adore you

Effortlessly lowering

Lower down the shaft

At some point I hear you

you're taking forever because I'm last in the
crew **ROPE FREE!**

The Deepest Journey
I ever took

The days have all aged out, drained.

My little paws felt frozen at first,

for icy water pulsed through veins

hardening tarred heart, now shrunken, wrin-
kled

But I decided to take this journey

alone.

Running thoughts of hope that never followed

fake nostalgia of memories never to return.

but they conjure in caverns that echo

Echo over in my skull

takes my lust

strip me from love

drown me in thoughts

harshly ringing in ears

coming back to mind

infecting my eyes

filling up my time

Being, severed

-apart.

And then

thoughts had left

water that once terrified me

became soothing

lick and lap me up

Warmth beating my heart

and drain me from hurt.

honey energy

heaping in my soul

light up grey walls

sharp edges become a fine line to walk on

Who you thought I was

is no longer here.

Alone.

Opening up cracked and stained window eyes

lighting up each room with electric energy

running my thoughts and ideas through each
corridor

like an unstoppable, hidden metronome:

each strike unleashing my goddess in the privacy of darkness.

Stagnant corners etched in darkness forever

No matter how much light I cautiously shine,

it cannot reflect onto those parts of past.

And yet-

The power of understanding those unkempt edges

gives me hope: I cannot waste my energies there!

I must light up!

Light up what I can!

No stalactite or trench left untouched!

I am alone.

But for the first time,

I am seen!

Tip toeing beneath your feet

waiting for the right time to free myself from
this hole

But now I can finally hear my own thoughts

so let me stay a while longer...

for I am no longer waiting to be found.

Orange

Orange is your teethy smile that I felt as you pressed your lips against mine

Orange is our eyes closed in darkness as senses filled, but lungs decline

Orange are my breasts, pushed against while icy water flows in my thighs

Orange as fingers glide up my hips and wrap round my waist, hands alight

Orange is the whimper and moan drowned out by waters that ebb and tide

Orange is the colour of you pushing and pressing into me, pants now tight for Orange does not belong in caves,

unless the iron, forged, does tint the water so,
like pastels on a white sheet

and Orange is not seen in this black pit of pur-
gatory,

as our naked skin was not meant to lather over
and tumble in mud.

but here; with me, is Orange:

that divulges my sensitivity

decisively opens my legs

and pulls at my hair

and whispers in my ears

and peels back my skin

piece by piece

until white small strings

that cover my juicy, young, plump heart

are left loose in your open hands

and the fresh tangy smell that drifts over your
nose

leaves your mouth watering-

to devour

until you finish.

the orange is squashed bare, seeds opened up

and scattered in this cavern

until the once citrus and sickly sweet,

is now a stench that sticks on the walls and floor,

growing more repulsive each day

until they turn a shade of green.

White flecks of fluff grow as you abandon the
scene.

The place where you skinned and opened me up

was now just a place where we had once fucked.

The truth I have
come to find

I will never prusik up Titan.

And for many years I thought,

that I might,

but being too scared of heights

it may be something I never do.

I may never be athletic as I wanted to be

and for such a time I believed,

I could walk for 10 hours straight

until I trained and realised,

I needed more tea breaks

than the others.

What a shame,

I thought.

But it's ok.

I may never walk the caves less travelled

and fly to far away countries

to map the new charters of the world

where the virgin caves are pristine

But I prefer the feeling

of the well-travelled cave

and the paths I begin to know

through history of their past wonderers

and are detailed on aged maps

Once I perhaps pushed myself too much to im-
press those others

with me on trips

whilst my anxiety dripped

into my bloodstream

but now I have learned my limits.

The line between enjoyment

and

Anxiety

is a well-learned skill deserved only by those who;

know not to fool themselves into pushing boundaries

only for they

themselves,

to break.

Small Balls

There is nothing like that feeling of..

...well...

how do I say this?

diving in the icy water,

wading through the muddy pond

in complete darkness

because perhaps you feel slightly pressured to by your friends.

(even so- it is the only way toward adventure!)

But then the water seeps through into your pants

and soaks through your privates

soaks past them like your privates were never there in the first place

and now they're numb in pale ice- perhaps they've gone forever?

When finally, the water drains as you stand out of pond, shivering:

And you realise-

That the only way back out the cave is to wade through it all once again.

An ode to darkness

a bleak sense that envelopes the soft fibres of my face

pricking me numb in the cool air that floats around our warm bodies,

forgetting my fingers exist, indifferent to my being

and eyes wide open to envelope the images in my brain.

I give into you with a sudden

!flinch!

as you shroud me in the feeling of quiet,

for the presence of your absence rings loudly in my ears and freezes my senses

and the suspicion that someone, - *something* – might shift within your stagnant realm

up against my face, anything could be there, but I only guess from what I saw before time itself stops to gaze upon you in awe, and deep chasm vibrations course through

I cannot escape the feeling that you have been following me for a while now

and that I was prey to you all along. I know one day I must live with you.

whilst it is calmer in your kingdom, I must flee back to my own

whilst it was nice sitting in your wisdom, I turn my light on, so!

Mother red in
tooth and claw

Her glazed marble eyes gazed upon her Mother as she clung onto the earthly clothes that she bore:

"When will he come back?" She muttered.

Mother looked upon her child tenderly with a proud and loving smile:

"He may never come back, my child- he might as well be lost in those caverns, for all we know."

Her eyes welling up at the sound of those softly flying words, landing in her ears like soft dandelion seeds, tapping the grass as they fly across the light wind of the summer meadow. Mother, rooting her hands onto the girl's head, soft and silent as moss:

"Oh my, a cat *has* got your tongue, hasn't it?

But can you not see? Maybe we will never find him again, as he *chose* to walk into those caves, but do you remember the times shared? Precious moments you may keep in the memory of your soul. Remember you are the woman that fed that cat - but now no amount of food can usher its return, for this is the way of his will. And a cat cannot be convinced against his own will!"

The small girl lowered her head, closed her eyes, and Mother continued:

"You miss this dear cat- how are the times you stroked his hair and kissed his forehead whilst he played on your lap! But you are also content enough to keep the lap warm for yourself. I have seen you love yourself in many ways that most cannot. That is the power I gave you long before your time here."

Her little limbs now standing up straighter, taller, in her small tear-soaked pinafore dress, she looked Mother straight in the eyes:

"Please just one thing, Mother, more than anything else: Is my little cat dead?"

Mother glanced down one last time, raising a bushy eyebrow in annoyance:

"*He is not.*

My child- The whole of your life waits for you, and you must make haste into planning and writing out your next chapter. I have seen strength of a thousand beans within you, and for this I say: the energy in your heart far outweighs the hurt that you have long suffered. You are ready now, ready to storm through the beauty that I have created for you. Do not wait for him any longer, when he knows the way back to you very well. Focus yourself and I will be here, watching your roots grow and your flowers, flourish."

The Peak District

Once upon a time there was a large slab of rock
named The Peak District.

And what a beauty she was-!

Young and unmoving

her thick and rolling hills

covered by enchanting trees

she called and called

until young men settled around her

viewing her soft locks and kissing her

young grey walls.

over time she did age and wither-

Her once large bosom now hallowed out

her wrinkled large crevices and cracks

still calling from afar to long lost men

who rest in her rolling blankets

and camp in her hidden valleys

as she bodes them to sleep.

The first men who had walked her,

are now long gone,

but the fresh young flesh that discover her new caves

respect and caress each bump and each lump she has

and watch the water as it trickles down her throat

carving out her life in the shadows

oh! the stillness of her lakes and the hush of her storms

how men long to stay with her for one night more..

and so you, dear reader:

she calls you to her limestone and battered cloudy skies

as beady cars cut through her snaking paths

that gaze upon her in awe and wonder;

she calls you to the hidden village under the lake

and the hole of the elves, beckoning pit of death

and the large gouge in stone that towering giants forged

and the water of the good goddess that gives from ground

and after thousands of years, men still chant for her;

deep within the beating heart of Yorkshire

forever in her rocking chair- grandmother of nature

she sits and waits

like a poker player foreseeing her hand of cards

but never allowing us the relief of laying them down

so we may only stare in awe of her deep fine lines

as her colourless eyes watch our wandering feet, like a mirror

only she may know the fortune of the bed she has made.

from the heavy seas of the past, that almost drained her out

to the falling of winnat's pass, or the building of Kinder Scout

it is the high winds that batter our hearts dry with love-

for you,

my dear,

The Peak District.

The Fragile Cave

If wonder lust has brought me home

then it's safe to dark cave, return.

Though fragile in life, still a mess-

but not slave of memories left

The unkempt garden under bright day's sky

with thick ivy, and God's swift butterflies

closes upon the dark rift that pulls me in

from the path that I built from my own sin

birds that sing and sun that sits upon cheek
burns white skin brightly, upon dark shade seeks
with crack'd and cold inviting entrance speaks
the empty shade calls closer with its creaks

now with wooden sign: never again; I implor'd!
the wrong feet had trodden this way before
and so 'only open to myself' written now
upon my secret fragile cave, lost, now found.

I pace through the walls that had once caved in,
only now to be found more peaceful within
In further, the stone wraps around my curves
whilst cave pearls sit pretty, and time stops its turns

to build love like a stalagmite takes many years
with water droplets building from hope,
dreams, truths, fears.

to thrash it from the root would make it fall, crumble,

but! the calcite still exists, perhaps now humbled.

It can't be turned back into water whence it came

Nor can love be unloved, I cannot unspeak your name.

Or memories: built high, we founded together

Now sitting on the floor in pieces, forever

I took the shards of stalagmite home with me,

kept them in my pocket, where your smile used to be.

Rummaging my hands through trousers, evr'y time,

cutting me softly as I fingered them fine

I sat them in the palm of my scarred hands,
bare

I showed them to others and cried in despair

I tried to glue them back together at night

but I will never own all the pieces; in spite.

I put all the pieces into a small box,

and put it away in a corner in the loft

the box collected dust, and scars of past remain

the lessons they gave me, we'll never be the
same!

But now, sat in my warm fragile cave, alone,

Soft light pouring in, flowing and draping gown

Thank god my hands have healed up just in
time!

To fix the fragile cave that I left far behind

Thank you for reading. Many months of passion, love and hard work was put into this book. I hope you enjoyed it. If you feel you enjoyed this book tremendously, then please leave a nice review, or lend this book to others so that they may feel the joy of a well-loved book! This book was for all cavers, now and in the future.

About the Author:

Elise Freshwater-Blizzard is a current under-graduate studying Linguistics and English Language at the University of Sheffield. She is due to graduate in the year 2021. She is also a proud member of Sheffield University Speleological Society, and Sheffield Poetry Society. She is highly interested in the preservation of nature, and has filmed a series of documentaries based on caves and caving for a non-caving audience called 'Deep Down Under'. She is also passionate about writing her thoughts down, Buddhist practice and pushing her fears to new heights.

Connect with Elise on:

Intagram: elisefrehwaterblizzard

Youtube: Elise Freshwater Blizzard

About the cover artist:

Rae Robinson is a Sheffield based tattoo artist.

<u>Connect with Rae on:</u>

Instagram: @raerobinsontattoo

Email: tattoosbyrae@gmail.com

Website: **<u>raerobinsontattoo.bigcartel.com</u>**

Lightning Source UK Ltd.
Milton Keynes UK
UKHW012115300520
364101UK00002B/378

9 781838 532673